When I
Meet Myself

—

Shahida Alvarado

Published by Amethyst Horizon Publishing
Michigan- USA
ISBN: 978-1-9711129-02-0
Printed in the United States of America.

For Luis
whose love makes everything possible.

Contents

Part I — When I Meet Myself

When I meet myself

She will come knocking hard at the door—
pounding her way inside.

When I meet myself...
she will stand tall in front of me,
chest lifted,
her bosom rising to my chin,
her gaze piercing straight into my soul.

She will stare me down
and watch my face fold into a frown.
Our eyes will meet—
locked tight.

I will not move.
Movement would turn my back to her,
and I refuse to return to the journey I was
on.

I will stand tall,
feet planted deep into the ground.

When I meet myself—
I will not be ready.
No, I won't.

But she will come pounding anyway,
forcing her way to the door.

When I meet myself—
she will say without words:

You are ready.
Bring on the tears.
Let them flow.
Bend your knees if you must,
but don't you dare turn on your heels.

When I meet myself,
it won't be on the floor—
no, it won't.

I will be standing at the door,
spine strong,
breath steady,
ready to follow this new life
with strength,
courage,
bravery,
and all.

Architect of Dreams

I am the architect of my dreams.
My thoughts of becoming — of changing
of living what I imagine to be my best life
rise and manifest as structures in my mind.
At night, I fall asleep exhausted
from the building and planning —
the work of shaping a life I have not yet lived
but already carry within me.

Before sunrise, my mind wakes my body
 and sets to work again —
laying foundations that sometimes feel impossible
 yet somehow remain strong.

Layer after layer,
I add the exteriors and interiors
until it feels complete —
though I know completion will never exist,
because I am always changing,
always dreaming.

Some days I want to break and tear down
everything I've built.
I pause and think.
Maybe I need to restart—
simplify
or complicate —
whatever my soul requires.

So, I begin again,
mind, body, soul, and spirit
working together
to build — build — build
and rebuild —
the architecture of my dreams.

The Witness

A shadow sits in the early hours beside the sea,
waiting for the sun to rise over the horizon.
The shoreline holds her like an old friend—
still, quiet, safe—
as the waves move in their slow morning rhythm.

Her feet hover inches above the chilled saltwater and pebbles,
 a softness touching a hardness,
 a reminder that contrasts can coexist.
Is she here for the sun, or for the water?

I watch from a distance
as she wraps her arms around her shoulders,
a shawl cocooning her from something unseen.
This is her ritual—
 the same place, the same hour, the same silence.
Perhaps she waits to witness the moment
when the rising sun meets the sea,
when its reflection becomes a path of gold
that only early souls get to walk upon.

Perhaps she longs to be the sun—
a beam of light that radiates across worlds,
warming what it touches,
 painting beauty for those who choose to rise with it.

Or maybe she wishes to be water—
 to move without permission,
 gentle or wild, soft or fierce,
to fill every space without losing herself.

Water can soothe.
Water can overwhelm.
Water is always enough.
Why does she sit and stare?
Is she the sun or the water, or both?
Her presence feels heavy, wrapped in quiet despair.

Emotional War

It feels like war unfolds itself inside the dark room.
The sound of nearby snoring is the only unsettling noise,
and to the naked eye
the occupied bed looks peaceful.
Night brings calm to the air.
The only natural movement
should be between the stars and the moon—
shifting, making space for the sun to rise.
But a silent war takes place
between the mind and the body.
Wake up, the body says to the mind.
Let's go to work.
So much is left undone.
And the mind pleads, exhausted:
Leave me alone.
Let me be.

But the body is restless.
It will not stop moving,
disturbing the peace
that the night has created.

War comes and goes
now and then,
but sometimes the mind
is too determined,
forcing the body to rise
before it is ready—
forming a pattern of chaos.
Not always,
but more than enough
to make peace feel distant.

Morning arrives,
and mind and body
almost align,
work together again—
seeking peace,
knowing the sun
will soon make space
for the moon and stars,
and maybe
the war will unfold
again.

Wrapped in a Cocoon

The room was silent.
A gentle, calm voice whispered,
Lay down... It's time to pause.
Palms to the sky,
heart wide open,
eyes closed.

I can feel the sound of my heart,
the warmth of my breath.
I am paused—
not alone,
but safe on my mat.
Breathe,
the voice whispers,
in and out...

My chest feels lighter
with every inhale and exhale.
I can surrender to this moment.

I am here now—
and that is all that matters.
Then, taken off guard,
the voice grows louder
yet somehow calmer,
spilling a story into the air:

A butterfly
 who lay for a while
inside a cocoon...
and when ready,
 crawled its way back
 onto the earth.
I listen with quiet interest.

My heart takes a leap.
Tears begin to fall.
The words are strength.
They reach me.
They become me.
I feel like that butterfly—
years spent inside a cocoon,
and now

I have crawled out of my shell,
still trying to find my feet
 so I can stand tall.
The tears keep rolling.
This delicate creature,
 fluttering through the world,
 moving between flowers,
 camouflaged by nature—
 can grow so strong.

It can withstand its becoming,
and have the patience to know
when the right time comes
to finally fly.

The Horizon

Hope rises every morning.
Gone is the night... yesterday has passed.
A new day arrives—Hope lifts itself over the horizon,
coloring the sky in yellows, oranges, and purples.
Hope becomes a glowing sphere of new beginnings.
Look and witness the power of thought.
A new day stands before you—take it with no attachments,
only the chance to begin again.

Do not carry past days forward or
let them change their color.
This new light paints itself in the colors of now... here.
Stand in its strength and pause.
Stop.

Close your eyes and inhale.
Exhale past days—regret, shame, fear...
whatever names you give them.
Let them go.
Inhale the horizon.
Accept its invitation to begin with hope.

My Routine Is My Anchor

People may not understand,
and honestly — that's fine.
I don't need to justify the pain I chase,
the early mornings that feel like mine.

When the world is quiet,
and dawn is barely a line of light,
I lift and sweat in the silence —
my body steady, my spirit tight.
These early hours hold me
when life moves far too fast,
when choices sit heavy on my chest,
and peace slips from my grasp.

My routine becomes my anchor —
keeping me grounded, holding me near,
pulling me back from drifting,
clearing the weight of fear.
grateful I didn't let go,
grateful I didn't disappear.
This routine — this sacred rhythm —
my quiet, steady guide.

Take a Breath

When you feel like hope is slipping away,
pause.
Take a deep breath.
Begin again.
Breathe hope into your thoughts...
let go,
and exhale.

And when you feel lost,
return to the one thing
that never leaves you—
your breath.

A Blessed Road

The road chose me—
I did not choose it.
My feet resisted every step,
heavy with questions,
aching with why.
Time led the way,
and I followed—impatient, unsure,

My gaze stayed fixed ahead,
too afraid to turn back,
afraid I would pause too long
and lose the road before me.

Then one day,
light found my eyes.
What once felt dark
revealed itself—
every bend, every turn
carrying new possibility.

What I feared as punishment
unfolded into a passage.
And the road I walked unwillingly
became a symbol
of blessing.

Strong Like a Soldier

Life requires readiness,
the way soldiers train
for battlefields.

Discipline cannot be explained—
only practiced.

This way of thinking is necessary,
even when it looks
like madness.

Life is not a war,
but it can break you
without warning.

Unprepared, doors stay open to chaos,
and you become the casualty
of your own choices.

Stay ready.

A soldier—for life's unexpected battles.

A Birthday

A new life takes its first breath
as love and joy swell inside a hospital room.
The newborn's cry breaks the silence,
bringing tears to the woman waiting
to wrap her arms around the human
she carried for months—
her womb, the first home.

A child arrives
in a world of billions,
yet claims a place that belongs to no one else.
Birth reminds us that though we are different,
we share one truth:
we all entered through the same doorway—
born into a place,
within a story not yet written.

Born to become...
the quiet thread that ties us all.
And as the years unfold,
with every age and every candle,
a birthday remains—
a reminder of that distant room
where a newborn first cried,
first inhaled,
and began.

Freedom

The door feels like it's calling me—
inviting me to walk through.
My feet feel too grounded.
The foundation beneath me has weakened,
yet I remain standing,
choosing strength even when it trembles.

An unspoken voice lingers in the air,
unfinished memories holding me
longer than I intend to be there.
If I leave too soon,
my absence becomes time without closure—
moments left unresolved.

Freedom waits on the other side,
quiet and patient,
until I decide
to loosen my grip,
let go,
and walk through.

The Role of a Mother

Have you ever stopped to think about this role — Mother?
Its title, its weight, its endless responsibilities.
Have you noticed how the hardest job in the world
 is often the one taken for granted by everyone else?
To step into this role,
 a woman must carry the weight of another human being
before she ever holds them in her arms.

She makes a quiet promise to herself and to the world:
 I will give my time.
 I will share my life.
 I will sacrifice my tears,
 my emotions,
 and even my thoughts
 to raise not one child,
 but perhaps more.

She follows a path walked by billions before her,
yet somehow the journey feels completely new.
Her own life slips gently into the back seat,
 and the human she helped bring into this world
becomes the priority.

Have you ever sat in the presence of this role
and whispered to yourself,
I a Mother

Or do the days blur into days —
routines, chores, the steady rhythm of "getting on with life" —
until babies become toddlers,
toddlers become teenagers,
and the roles keep shifting?
and through every change,
there you are — constant.
Loving.
Protecting.
Caring.

Sometimes invisible,
not because you are unseen,
but because you are always there —
the driver of the journey,
yet also the passenger
in the life you brought into the world.

Then one day,
Time sweeps you off your feet again,
and you must let go.

You must give wings
to the adult standing in front of you —
with their own opinions, their own voice,
their own understanding
and perhaps even their own judgments
of the job you did.
And still,
you remain a Mother.
A constant.
A beginning and a safe return.
A role that requires everything
and gives back in ways words can barely hold.

Filled with Gratitude

Gratitude always comes to my mind.
It rises before the sun,
soft and steady,
like breath after a long-held silence.
Gratitude keeps my heart full—
let my tears fall without fear,
lets my chest open
to the truth of where I stand now
versus where I could have been.

Sometimes the realization alone
makes my body sink into relief—
a quiet, trembling exhale
that whispers,
 I made it through.
I am here now.
Not surviving.
Not pretending.
But here—fully, wholly, awake.

Gratitude keeps my feet grounded
when my past could have uprooted me.
It keeps my soul at peace
when life could have hardened me.
And every time I pause,
 every time I look at the path behind me
 and the horizon ahead,
 I know one truth:
Gratitude isn't just something I feel—
 it is the home I live in now.

Chasing the Sun

I am in love with sunset—
the way the sky shifts its colors
as if repainting all my sorrow
into something I can bear tomorrow.

I chase the sun.
I run up and down the hill,
searching for that single breath,
that quiet pause where time stands still.

The sun becomes my perfect peace,
my pace
on days when my thoughts refuse to cease,
when life presses heavily on my chest
and I fight so hard just to rise, to rest.

My longing for the sun is a hidden confession...
I chase it when I'm drowning
in the weight of my own tension.
I chase the sun
when shadows creep too close to me—
I chase the fading light
so it can chase the noise that will not let me be.

Broken Dreams

We met on the foundations of shared dreams—
visions of a colorful future
painted in possibility.
Hours of meaningful conversations
spilled between meals,
laughter lingering like warm steam in the air.
The excitement of the unknown
sat comfortably between us,
hearts full—
of love,
of hope,
with bravery standing guard at the door.
We believed it would be enough.
But we could not weather the storms of life.

The winds came faster than expected,
and the ground beneath us
began to crack.
Dreams shattered in front of our eyes,
splintering into sharp truths—
what once held promise
turned dark,
unfamiliar.
Nightmares replaced what we built.
Hidden truths surfaced.
Kept secrets unfolded.
And there we stood,
among the ruins,
learning that not every dream
was meant to last.

Words are Powerful

Words don't always come from the mind.
You may think they do—
but every sentence grows from a seed inside you,
rooting itself deep,
rising upward until it breaks the surface
and becomes sound.
Your words belong to you
and come from you,
but not always from the mind.

In anger, words rise from the heart—
mixed with sadness,
with disappointment—
and they manifest themselves
into tears.
Then suddenly,
words explode into sentences
that shake you like an earthquake of emotion.
Your body trembles,
your breath stumbles,
until you cannot stop.

No, your words do not come only from your mind.
Your heart hijacks reason and logic,
unwinding the past,
pulling old hurts into the present,
wrapping your words around moments
that served no one well—
not then,
not now.

Yet there you are,
trying to calm yourself
with logic,
with softness,
with steady breath—
but the heart will not give up
until every word
you have felt
has finally been set free.

Part II — The Horizon

Castaway

As the sun casts its glow across the water,
I shimmer beneath the surface—
buried in sand,
hidden under the sea.
I hear voices above me,
but no one sees me now.
Bright-colored tails brush past,
fish weaving through current,
nudging me gently
as I drift farther and farther away.

Once,
I was love between two connected souls—
a promise of forever.
But time changed me.
Happiness turned into sadness
as the years slipped by.
A silent storm brewed,
and memories of that special day,
at the very shore where I now rest,
return to me in waves.
I was home on her hand—
a precious place to be.
Until the day I was tossed violently
into the ocean
so no one could see me.
Now I lie here,
cast away—
a witness to what was lost,
a secret kept by the sea.

More Than a Woman

You are more than a woman.
The voice inside me screamed it loud—
again, again—
a truth unbowed.

October wrapped itself
in ribbons of pink,
reminding us of battles
far closer than we think—
women fighting for their lives,
families holding on to hope
like the last thread
of a fragile rope.

The battle is not over.
We are not done.
Our storms look different,
but pain touches everyone.
Your story, your journey,
your past and becoming—
you are a warrior rising,
a heart that keeps drumming.

You are not broken—
your light still burns bright.
Put life into living,
even with secret hurts
that nobody knows.

There will be days
when you feel you cannot live—
nothing left inside you,
nothing left to give.

But even then,
your spirit won't fall—
because a woman begins
where others end—
you rise through it all.
Hope lives in you—
quiet, unspoken,
still breathing.

Goodbyes

The day has arrived—
no more tomorrows.
Memories rise to meet me,
softening the sorrow,
wrapping me in moments
I no longer borrow.

They hold me steady
so I do not fall,
even when time feels like a friend—
offering nothing at all.

The sun keeps rising
and setting on my skin,
as days slip into days
and I feel the ache begins.

And then the moment comes
when we must part—
the hurt arriving before the tears,
with trembling hands,
and breaking hearts.

Family

I walked into a gallery
and saw the roots of a tree
 hanging from the ceiling.
The tree itself was nowhere in sight.
Its roots stopped me—
my breath cold,
my body still,
the room suddenly empty
except for me
and those tangled lines
 dangling like secrets.

I couldn't look away.
My family filled my thoughts.
Those roots—messy, interwoven—
looked just like us:
connected,
yet stretched wide across places
we no longer share.

The branches and leaves were missing,
 just as the years we grew together
now live out of sight—
memories unseen,
but still holding us,
still exposing us,
still tying us to one another
in ways only roots can.

The losses,
the pain,
the quiet love—
all the parts below the surface
that no one speaks of,
yet everyone feels.

And standing there,
beneath a tree I could not see,
I realized something gentle:
We are not only shaped
by the roots we come from—
we are also softened
by the courage to grow beyond them.

And maybe meeting myself
means meeting every part of them too:
the ones who came before me,
the ones who walk beside me,
the ones I carry forward
as new roots form
in the soil of my own becoming.

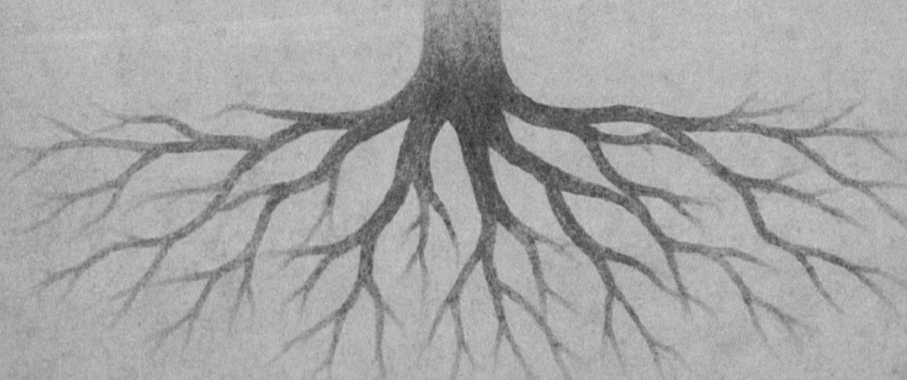

Hungry for Love

An empty space lives
in the quiet moments—
when the day ends
and there is no voice
to ask how it went.
The feeling of untouched skin
drifts through the air,
a memory of arms
that knew just where to rest,
of peaceful nights
held by the comfort of sleep,
without counting the distance
between two aching hearts—
promises shared
 through a cold, hard screen.

A hunger for love,
or to be loved.
A constant reminder—
the heart remembers
what closeness feels like,
what it means to be chosen,
to be held,
and to stay.
But even in the silence,
there is a quiet knowing—
that one day
love will find its way
and fill the empty corners
at the end of the day.

A Slow Heat

Stir me up like hot soup on a cold winter day,
feel my steam curl around your face
and pull you my way.

Sip me slow,
taste by taste,
let my warmth slip into the shadows
you never let go to waste.

Let me burn through the quiet ache,
soothe the pain you never name—
let my heat rise,
let me tame the flame.

Sip me slow until you're full,
let every memory linger and set—
hold me close,
and make me a taste
you never forget.

The Shadows

The city glitters in sleepless light,
busy even as midnight breathes.
But the hour knows the truth—
it is time to rest.

Still, two shadows move
through the fractured glow,
haunted by a wandering unrest,
walking where sleep cannot reach.

Cemented in Tears

My strength is power,
but you don't see me bleed.
Your eyes only see the walls I built,
but you are blind to the foundation beneath—
a foundation mixed with tears
that turned to cement,
so no one could break my heart.

You don't see the wounds
I learned to hide.
You don't see
 that my heart hurts too.

Your words have the power
to rip me apart—
that is why I've learned
to disguise my pain
and look the other way.

My eyes carry truths
no one ever tried to see.
Behind all my strength,
I am human—
and I bleed too.

Torn Shoes

Do you think you could walk
a mile in my shoes?
Shoes torn open with emotional bruises,
heels tired from roads
I never wanted to choose.

These shoes are too heavy
for another soul to bear—
they've wandered foreign lands,
chasing truths
buried deep in unfamiliar air.

My shoes belong to me,
and only my feet know the scars they hide,
the stories stitched in silence,
the ghosts that travel at my side.

Their history is priceless—
a weight only I can use.
No other heart,
no other soul,
could ever fit inside my shoes.

Home

Home carries feeling—
spaces where souls meet.
Home is not brick and mortar,
nor stones beneath our feet.

Home is where your spirit feels free,
where the mind rests in gentle peace.
Home is where you meet yourself—
and finally release.

Part III — Love, Loss, and the Roles We Carry

I Choose Me

Not because I was unseen,
but because they never learned
how to see me deeply—
even at ground level.

I stood close.
I spoke softly.
I gave without noise.
Still, my presence passed through
like light on a closed window.

The pain stayed tangled
when I waited to be met
where I already was.
So, I stopped reaching outward
 for recognition
and began the quiet work
of self-anchoring.

I learned to hold my own weight,
to name my own becoming,
to witness the depth
without needing an audience.
I do not rise in spite.
I rise in truth.
Choosing myself
was not an ending—
it was my new beginning.

My Heart

You are the keeper of my pain,
offering no judgment, no refrain.
My companion when I felt alone,
holding my hand when nights felt too cold.

You helped me build my boundaries,
when times were sharp and unforgiving,
when explanations were unnecessary,
and silence was still living.

When I could not name what I was feeling,
you stayed—steady, revealing nothing.
I learned to slow down—
without disappearing.
You beat steadily, not loud,
so you can hear my whispers,
soft enough to calm my tears.

Beautiful Body

Soft, jazzy music keeps me company.
The night feels smooth against my skin.
The mirror echoes—
you look beautiful.

My body dances softly,
curves and imperfections
left at the door,
uninvited on the dance floor.
My body arrives
before judgment.

The restaurant hums with hunger,
patrons ready to feast.
The menu does not measure worth.
Food becomes pleasure
without guilt.
No numbers.
No apologies.

Deliciousness arrives on a plate—
an invitation to celebrate my body and soul.

Stained Age

Age feels stained by years of living—
by lessons of success and failure
that carved their wisdom into bone.

Like pages of an old, battered book,
creased, marked, once tossed aside,
 yet holding truths worth rereading.

Age connects the soul to the body—
a quiet remembrance,
a soft returning,
a new becoming.

Become Like Water

Flow gently where you can,
slip through unseen spaces,
move without resistance.

Let softness be your strength.
Let patience guide you on
past sharp tongues
and heavy hands.

But always remember—
water is not weak.

It claims space
through steady force.

When tested, it rises.
When pushed too far,
it grows into waves—
heavy, strong, undeniable.
Adapt, but do not shrink.
Choose how you flow.

Quiet Hours

Tired eyes
  carry the weight of midnight,
  while the mind wanders—
  bright, restless, alive.

Sleep is put on hold,
  not forgotten,
  as dreams are sketched
  in quiet hours.

These eyes are tired,
  but the vision
  is wide awake.

Moments

The moment will come
when life feels tangible—
when you long for simple days.
It will feel like your dreams
have been taken hostage.

Life will wrap around you so tightly.
You can't breathe.
Your heart will thump,
waiting for a moment
when you can exhale
and inhale life again.

The moment will come
when you must choose—
to love, to live,
to be grateful.
And still,
life will try
to take those feelings hostage.

But you will stand—
with your truest self,
with your chosen people—
and say:
I choose to stand in this moment,
for all the years to come.

Deep Underground

Rests the bones of a man who felt the world threw stones—
no matter how he tried.
Buried secrets
between a husband and a wife,
lives expired,
truths conspired,
words unspoken shaped a life.

Deep underground,
the truth now fades,
rotting gently where the cold earth lies.

No one will know
the crooked path to wealth and fame,
nor whisper who was set to blame.
Flesh has fallen,
dust to dust—
bones surrendered back to rust.

The soul stayed near,
or so the earth made clear.

Unplanned Writing

My writing is unplanned—
judge me if you will—
I say my writing is unplanned.
No ideas prepared,
no overthinking,
just words born from a tired, withered soul...
a life lived on repeat,
a life unfolded,
a journey into becoming.

My writing is unplanned—
is that so hard to understand?
Words with meaning,
sentences threaded deep inside me,
 flowing like water—
 sometimes a storm
 wiping out everything in its path,
 other times so gentle
 it brings tears to my eyes.

Why do I write
with so much wisdom,
so much strength,
yet it feels raw—
like I'm digging into my own core
My writing is unplanned.

It rises from feelings and thoughts
I dare to share,
so I write quickly,
letting it pour out
before fear or doubt can tear me apart.

My writing is unplanned—
it paints pictures of color,
like the sun rising in its glory,
the kind that makes you stare
and whisper, that is beautiful.

Part IV — What Remains

Have You Ever Looked at the Trees?

Have you ever stopped and looked at the trees?
Or better—lie down, let your tired mind ease.
The world softly changes when your head meets the ground,
and your gaze lifts upward, where quiet truths are found.

The trees stand tall, guardians of air and sky,
branches leaning on branches as the seasons pass by.
They weave their shadows in patterns against the sunlight —
a silent art show whispered through leaves.

Have you ever wondered how a delicate seed,
buried and hidden, rose to meet your every need?
How it pushed through the earth with a patient, steady grace,
to grow into shelter—your calm, your safe place?

So, you could breathe in its beauty, rest under its shade,
find peace in the pathways its green hands have made.

Have you ever paused, even once, to feel all of this?
To notice the wonder that we so often miss.

November Is on My Back

It's shadow bending my knees,
pushing me low—
a weight I can't ignore
as the year hums behind the door.

It reminds me
to finish what I started.
I won't carry unfinished plans
into a new year.

It wakes me before my body is ready,
chains me to blue light,
forces a choice
between rest and deadlines.
November won't slow down.
Time does not soften.

So I rise.
I focus.
Whatever it takes—
I step forward, unfinished no more.

An Act of Kindness

An act of kindness
caught my eye,
as I sat above the street so high—
sipping warm coffee,
letting time drift by,
searching for a moment
to breathe... to sigh.
Below me, an old man stumbled and fell,
a sudden scene that woke me up.

My breath caught sharply,
my coffee nearly spilled—
life tilting in a heartbeat,
my balance almost tipped.
But two passing teens,
with nothing to gain,
paused their pace
 in the middle of the lane.
No hesitation,
no pride, no show—
just steady hands
and hearts that know.

They lifted him gently,
helped him stand tall,
as kindness still matters
in a world so small.
And from where I sat,
coffee warming my hands,
I felt hope rising
in quiet, golden strands.
A simple moment,
soft and unplanned—
reminding me of goodness
still walks this land.

Alone

Loneliness can steady my thoughts
or drown me in them.
Alone again—
no one to talk to
except the voices in my mind
as my fingers scroll
one reel after another,
passing time.

Alone with my thoughts—
a frightening place,
yet somehow
the silence can become a gift,
a small doorway
to self-discovery.

A Mother's Wish

See me—
see beyond the title of who I am.
A woman who was once a young child too,
a person with feelings.

My thoughts and emotions swim deep inside me,
each one shaped and colored
like fish beneath the sea.

Yet there are places no one can reach,
not even me—
too deep, too dark,
too dangerous to breathe.

See me—
not just as a home,
not only when you need something.
See me on the bright days too,
when laughter radiates like sunlight—
share that warmth with me.

Don't take my time for granted.
As the years pass,
so does my age.
Love me when love feels impossible,
when you question who I am.

Remember—
raising a child is not easy.

Forgive me
when I don't know how to ask.
Accept my mistakes
as lessons I am still learning.

Find gratitude in the years we shared:
the meals I prepared,
the moments I stayed,
the time I gave to watch you grow.

See me—
see the life we shared,
and the love that held it together..

Brewed Memories

He told me stories of coffee—
how he loves the smell,
but what he really loves
is the morning it carries.

A small table along a busy street,
observing those who pass by...
an unfolded newspaper,
an unfinished crossword.

Steam rising like his patience,
the sound of a hard brew.
The café knew his name.
The cup was always the same—
latte, the start to his day.
Time moved slower back then.

His grandfather sat across from him—
not saying much,
just being there.

His love of coffee feels
like a treasured memory searching for him.
A freshly brewed cup always finds him,
and suddenly he is younger,
reflecting on those old days,
listening without knowing—
he was learning how to stay.

That memory grew roots,
settling deep inside.
It became a dream—
to serve more than a drink,
to offer a pause, a moment to think.

A place where mornings feel held,
where stories are poured quietly
into waiting cups,
where memories continue
to warm us.

My Country

My heart holds me tight—
tears fill an emptiness
I never knew existed.
I am back again.

My country stayed,
waiting patiently for my return.
The land where I took my first breath.
On bended knees—

I grasp the sand between my fingers
and look toward the horizon—
open arms
waiting for me.

This ground knew my name
before I learned to speak it.

I have borrowed myself
to other lands,
but my country is where my name
was spoken
before I had words
to understand
what gratitude is,
or how it feels
to come home.

Part V — Choosing the Self

Quiet Strength

Life gathers us
in moments no one sees,
when the soul feels empty—
tired and worn.
Yet we choose to stay,
to pause,
to breathe.
Not for applause.
Not for recognition.
Not to be held up
by borrowed approval.

There is no performance—
no stage, no clapping hands,
only the truth
of quiet strength
that fills us
to live a life that matters.

To know
it is more than enough
to simply
be.

Awakened by Distance

Dreams of travel
turned into beautiful memories
of crossing borders—
watching unfamiliar horizons unfold.
Foreign lands became my teacher,
showing me how to see the world
through different eyes.

Travel lets the body flow
to the rhythm of life—
to languages that roll differently
on the tongue.

Memories become gifts:
scents, flavors, experiences
wrapped beautifully inside of you.

The body awakens—
footsteps on new ground,
sand between your feet,
water moving around you,
as you learn
how arrival feels.

Nervousness

The audience waits patiently
to witness months of practice—
late nights obsessing over perfection,
exhausted moments,
and everything else
that has found its way onto the stage.

They sit in silence,
waiting to experience the sound
that was perfected
when no one was around
to see how much work it took to get here.

But nervousness grips you tight,
stealing your breath,
making you feel weak.

Time freezes—
suspended between perfection and mistake.
Breathe, you think. Just be.
But nervousness won't let go.

It kidnaps your performance
and holds it hostage
in front of a silent audience,
waiting for the curtain to fall.

Tears Without Shame

Tears fall
without apology,
without carrying
the weight of the world
on fallen backs.

They are not wounds,
not scars left by life,
but the strength of healing—
not signs of breaking.
Tears wash away
 hidden pains.

Unscarred by bitterness,
untouched by fear,
these tears carry release,
not regret.

Soft, gentle cries—
and in that softness,
they become whole, not unbroken.

When I Speak My Truth

It is never just words from a life story.
It is the gathering of feelings and thoughts
that rise from the deepest core of my soul—
from the place where my spirit rests
between its dark days and its light.

When I speak, it comes from a bleeding heart,
from moments that have washed my pain clean
through tears of grief that have filled me up—
in places no one has seen,
so no one can make me feel empty again.

My truth is my space—
a life I have lived,
a past carved inside me
through memory
and fragile moments
I carry within me.

I Made It

The words echo.
Tears fall—
my body trembles,
unable to be still.
My emotions look confusing,
but this—
this is relief.

Relief that I survived.
I made it.
I breathe deeply,
steadying the shake,
quieting the storm
that once lived in my chest.

I made it—
shouting into the empty room,
my voice meeting the walls
that once heard my prayers
and saw my tears.

In the darkest moments life threw at me,
I stood.
I fought with strength—
with my own declaration:
I will love myself,
no matter what.

The path was lonely.
Silent.
Unforgiving.
But it led me here.
And even then,
I felt a higher power—
hands unseen,
holding me when I could not hold myself,
protecting me,
keeping me safe.

I made it.
Tears fall again—
not from pain,
but from gratitude
for the life I have built:
on strength,
on patience,
on unexpected love.

No one sees the back end—
the breaking,
the rebuilding,
the nights I chose faith over fear.

Your life reflects only
what narrow eyes can see,
a surface truth,
a fragile illusion.
But I know.
And that is enough.

A New Chapter

I have been around stories of people declaring
that a new chapter has begun—
lives stretched across pages and pages
of an unwritten book.
Years of untold journeys,
filled with strength, pain, tears, happiness—
every emotion a body can hold.

I've heard the conviction in their voices,
the proclamation of their souls,
when they say, "It's a new chapter."
A becoming.
A life unfolding again.

And I think of my becoming—
my new chapter.
But will it truly be new?

If my life were a story, a novel,
would these pages feel fresh to the reader?
Or would my past—my memories, my emotions—
leave ripples and tears
in the chapters behind it?

Would my pages look like tea spilled,
rusted and weathered with time?

And when I close my book,
the contrast of these new pages
against my old, tea-stained ones—
would it still feel like a new chapter,
or simply a new beginning
written on the same
tea-stained pages of my life?

When I Meet Myself, I remember that every step, every loss, every quiet strength, every horizon crossed, and every choice made was never meant to perfect me, only to return me—again and again—to the truth of who I am becoming.

— Shahida Alvarado

About the Author

Shahida Alvarado was born in South Africa and has lived in Abu Dhabi since 2002. She brings over fifteen years of experience teaching in both private education and within the Ministry of Education, alongside a lifelong devotion to learning, reflection, and personal growth.

She is a 500-hour Yoga Teacher, Master Reiki and Sound Healing practitioner, and a certified Life Coach. Her work is rooted in the belief that healing, awareness, and self-understanding begin by listening inward—through the body, the breath, and the quiet spaces we often overlook.

Travel has shaped her deeply. Moving between countries, cultures, and ways of living has expanded not only her worldview, but her relationship with identity, belonging, and becoming. These experiences live quietly inside her writing.

When I Meet Myself was written as a pause—a place to sit with truth, tenderness, and self-recognition. This book is not meant to teach, instruct, or perform. It is an invitation to slow down, to feel, and to meet yourself honestly, wherever you are in your journey.

www.ingramcontent.com/pod-product-compliance
Lightning Source LLC
Chambersburg PA
CBRC090834120626
46547CB00011B/692